The Lord's Prayer

BIBLE CHAPTERS FOR KIDS

"Our Father, who art in heaven,"

We are praying to God. He is our loving father in heaven.

"Hallowed be thy name."

Hallowed means "holy" or "great."
It's like saying, "Your name is awesome!"

"Thy kingdom come,"

God's kingdom is a loving place to be.

"Thy will be done, on earth
as it is in heaven."

God wants us to live in peace
and with goodness, so that
earth will be like heaven.

"Give us this day our daily bread."

We trust God to give us what we need every day.

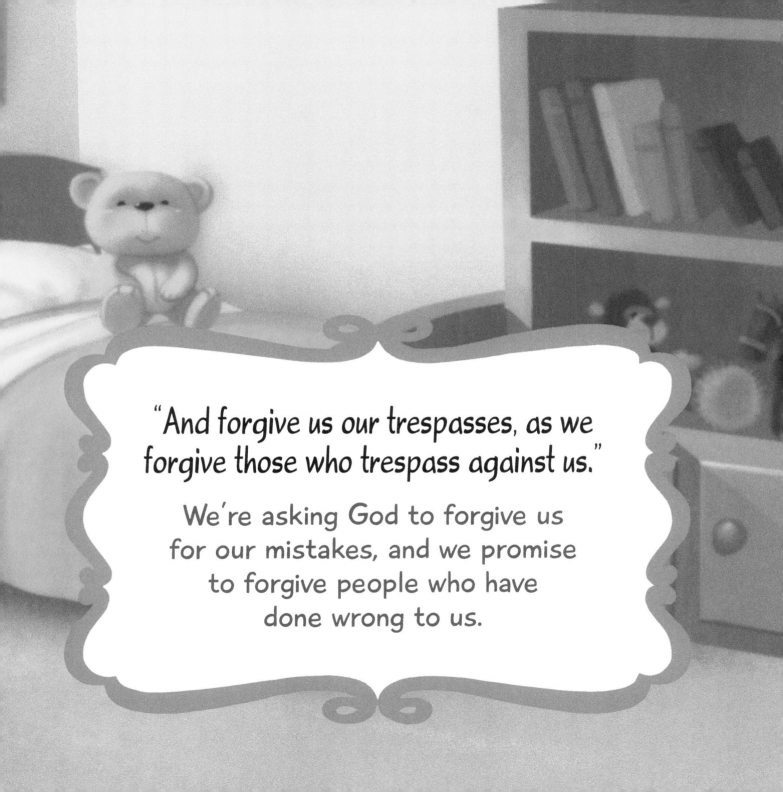

"And forgive us our trespasses, as we forgive those who trespass against us."

We're asking God to forgive us for our mistakes, and we promise to forgive people who have done wrong to us.

"And lead us not into temptation,
but deliver us from evil."

We're asking God to help us do the
right thing, even when it's hard to do.

"Amen."

Amen means "so be it,"
or "this is the truth and I agree."

Here are a few
prayers to use
throughout your day.

Dear God, we thank you for the night,
And for the pleasant morning light;
For rest and food and loving care,
And all that makes the day so fair.

- Rebecca Weston (1890)

Help us to do the things we should,
To be to others kind and good;
In all we do, in work or play,
To grow more loving every day.

- Rebecca Weston (1890)

Help me, Lord, to love you more
Than I ever loved before,
In my work and in my play
Please be with me through the day.

- Anonymous

God in heaven hear my prayer,
Keep me in thy loving care.
Be my guide in all I do,
Bless all those who love me too.

- Anonymous

Dear God, bless my little friends.
And bless my big friends too.
Help us to show lots of love
And grow up to be like you.

- Agnes de Bezenac

God, you are great and you are good,
And we thank you for this food;
Lord, by your hand we are fed,
Thank you for our daily bread.

- Anonymous

Thank you for the world so sweet,
Thank you for the food we eat.
Thank you for the birds that sing,
Thank you God for everything.

- Traditional

Now that the day is done,
I stop to think about you.
Thank you that you are near
So that I have nothing to fear.

-Agnes de Bezenac

Jesus, thanks for being here tonight,
I'm never out of your sight.
You're like a warm blanket over me.
That's just the way I like it to be.

-Salem de Bezenac

Now I lay me down to sleep,
I pray the Lord my soul to keep:
May God guard me through the night
And wake me with the morning light.

-Traditional

Jesus bless and Jesus keep me,
Guard me as I'm feeling sleepy.
Bless my dreams as I lay down;
Bless my loved ones all around.

-Salem de Bezenac

More titles in this series:

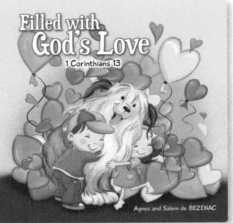

Published by iCharacter Ltd. (Ireland)
www.icharacter.org
By Agnes and Salem de Bezenac
Illustrated by Agnes de Bezenac
Colored by Sabine Rich.
Copyright 2012. All rights reserved.
ISBN 978-1-62387-113-0
All Bible verses adapted from the KJV.

CPSIA information can be obtained
at www.ICGtesting.com
Printed in the USA
LVHW082349040619
620182LV00016B/37/P